The Romberg Cello Sonata in E Minor

Practice Edition

A Learn Cello Practically Book

Written and Compiled by Cassia Harvey

CHP363

©2020 C. Harvey Publications
All Rights Reserved.
www.charveypublications.com - print books
www.learnstrings.com - downloadable books
www.harveystringarrangements.com - chamber music

Table of Contents

Section	Page
What's In the Book	3
How to Practice Using This Edition	4
Understanding Symbols and Terms	5
Reading and Playing Half and Whole Steps	6
Preparing to Play Romberg	7
Welcome!	8
Movement One - Preparatory Exercises	9
Movement One - With Study Notes	24
Movement Two - Preparatory Exercises	28
Movement Two - Written Slower for Counting	34
Movement Two - With Study Notes	36
Movement Three - Preparatory Exercises	38
Movement Three - With Study Notes	50

Sonata in E Minor - Complete Piece
- Movement One................56
- Movement Two................60
- Movement Three..............62

Sonata in E Minor - Cello Duet
- Movement One................66
- Movement Two................72
- Movement Three..............74
- Sonata (Cello II Part for Performance)......82

Sonata in E Minor - Piano Accompaniment
- Movement One................88
- Movement Two................94
- Movement Three..............97

Cello Curriculum Segments - Where to Place Romberg....106

What's In the Book

How to Practice Using This Edition
These pages have ideas for developing a practice strategy to learn the Sonata. From explanations of symbols and terms to a description of half and whole steps, these pages tell you how the book can be most helpful to you.

Preparatory Exercises
The most difficult parts in the Sonata were identified and then broken down and taught in these pages. The Preparatory Exercises for each movement are followed by the "Movement with Study Notes."

Movements With Study Notes
Each movement of the Sonata is written with notes for study, including marked positions, some beat marks, and extension reminders.

Complete Sonata
The entire cello part to the Sonata is here, for practice or performance.

Sonata with Cello Duet Part
The entire Sonata is included with a cello duet part that will allow you to practice or perform the piece with your teacher or with another cellist. If you'd like to perform the duet, the Cello II part is included by itself, after the score, so page turns can be easier.

Piano Accompaniment
The piano accompaniment, composed by G. Jansen, is included for study, practice, or performance.

Cello Curriculum Segment - Where to Place Romberg
These pages show how the Romberg Cello Sonata in E minor can fit in a cello curriculum, along with recommended methods, etudes, and supplemental study books.

How to Practice Using This Edition

1. Play and master the **Preparatory Exercises** for each movement.

2. You may also, at the same time, practice the piece using the **Movement with Study Notes** that follows each set of Preparatory Exercises.

3. Once you have learned the movement fairly well, transition to the same movement in the **Complete Piece** section (pages 56-65).

4. The entire book can be played with free **Play-Along** files. See below for more information.

5. Play the **Sonata with Cello Duet** part with your teacher or with another cellist.

6. If you know a pianist, play the sonata with the included **Piano Accompaniment**.

7. See what to play next in a typical cello curriculum, using the lists at the end of the book.

Play-Along Sound Files

Play-Along Sound Files for this book can be found at https://soundcloud.com/charveypublications/sets/the-romberg-cello-sonata-in-e.

The files are listed according to their page in the book.

Soundcloud can be accessed on your computer or on your mobile device, via their free app.

©2020 C. Harvey Publications All Rights Reserved.

Understanding Symbols and Terms

In this book, **Roman Numerals** indicate strings (never positions.)
I = A string, II = D string, III = G string, IV = C string

Beat marks are notated by a vertical slash | above some notes in the Preparatory Studies. In the Movements with Study Notes, small notes above the regular notes indicate how to subdivide for counting.

Positions are indicated by numbers and words: 4th position, 3rd position, etc.

Extend refers to reaching two whole steps with the fingers of the left hand. For more explanation of extensions, see a method such as Cello Stretching: Extended First Position (CHP243). Occasionally, an arrow will be used to remind you to extend forward or backward.
Closed refers to a regular position, where the hand is not extending.

Metronome markings are included in the Movements with Study Notes for both study and performance tempos. They are listed as a range (i.e. from 72-88). When you have learned the notes and bowings fairly well, you might want to start playing with the metronome and you can start at a quarter note = 72. As you progress, move the metronome up one or two notches and keep practicing. Continue getting faster until you reach the performance tempo where you feel most comfortable.

These markings are only approximate; feel free to play the piece at a slower or faster tempo!

Study Tempo: ♩=72-88   Performance Tempo: ♩=92-132

Alternate fingerings are sometimes included under the notes. In this case, pick the fingering that you prefer. You may also choose your own fingerings and bowings that are not included.

©2020 C. Harvey Publications   All Rights Reserved.

Reading and Playing Half and Whole Steps

Here are some practical ways to think of steps on the cello:
- The space between each finger in the regular (closed) lower positions is a half step.
- The space between three fingers (for instance 1st finger and 3rd finger) in regular (closed) lower positions is a whole step.
- To reach a whole step with 1st and 2nd fingers, you must extend or stretch. In this case, the thumb should move up under 2nd finger to allow you to reach easily.
- As you move up through the positions, the spaces between the notes get smaller. A half step in first position will be much bigger than a half step in seventh position.
- In the higher positions, both whole and half steps can be played by any two adjacent fingers (for instance 2nd and 3rd finger). Think of the half steps as "small spaces" and the whole steps as "big spaces" to help differentiate between the two.

Half steps are marked this way:

Half step space

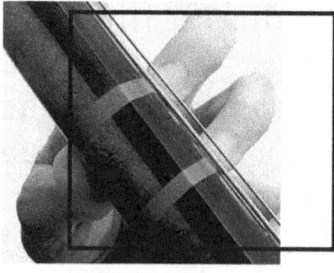

Whole steps are marked this way:

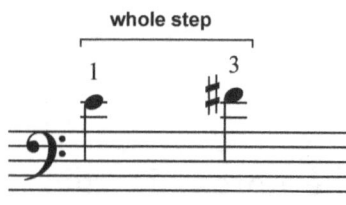

Whole step space with 1st and 3rd finger (closed postion.)

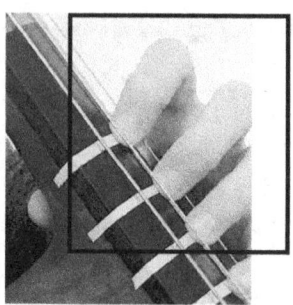

Whole step space with 1st and 2nd finger (extended position.)

©2020 C. Harvey Publications All Rights Reserved.

Preparing for Romberg

Prerequisite Skills for First Movement

- Reading and playing both closed and extended first position.
- Reading, shifting to, and playing in fourth position (including mid-string harmonic.)
- Reading, shifting to, and playing basic second and third position.
- Some familiarity with half position.
- Ability to play triplets, dotted quarter and eighth notes.

Prerequisite Skills for Second Movement

- See skills above.
- An ability to play some notes with vibrato.

Prerequisite Skills for Third Movement

- See skills above.
- Ability to play in a 6/8 time signature, including knowledge of how to count sixteenth, eighth, quarter, dotted quarter, and dotted half notes in this time signature.
- Familiarity with the concept of tenor clef. There is one measure with tenor clef notes in this movement, which are taught in the Preparatory Exercises.
- Knowledge of mid-string A harmonic so that you can shift to seventh position using this note as a guidepost.
- Ability to play a 3-Octave C major scale.

Recommended Books to Study Before Beginning the Romberg Sonata

- Fourth Position for the Cello (CHP131) or Fourth Position Study Method (CHPD078)
- Second Position for the Cello (CHP116)
- Third Position for the Cello (CHP116)
- The C Major Scale Book for Cello (CHP117) or the first four pages in Learning Three-Octave Scales on the Cello (CHP356).

Welcome!

Thank you for your purchase!

If you are happy with the book or have helpful information about it for other musicians and teachers, it would be super helpful if you could leave a review where you bought the book!

If you have a question about anything in this book, if there is anything you don't understand, or if there is anything you disagree with and you want to let us know, please reach out to us at charveypublications@gmail.com; we're happy to address your issue!

If there is any defect with the printed book, please know that we ourselves do not print the books. The best way to resolve a book printing issue is to contact the company where you purchased this book (or contact us if you purchased from www.charveypublications.com) for a full refund or exchange. If you discover a defect after the return window has closed, please notify the company so they can make appropriate changes at their printing facility and then contact us at charveypublications@gmail.com so we can help you to get a correctly printed copy of the book you can use.

Above all, we want your playing and teaching experience to be better because of our books. Suggestions, ideas, criticisms and positive comments are always welcome at charveypublications@gmail.com.

We realize that paperback binding is not ideal for sheet music, however it allows us to offer this, and all of our other books, for less than half as much as we would have to charge for different binding. If you'd like a downloadable copy of this book to play from a tablet or to print out, visit www.learnstrings.com and use code **printbookromberg** to get 30% off your purchase of a PDF copy.

And visit us at https://www.charveypublications.com/better-string-playing-blog for free sheet music that you might find helpful!

Here's to better string playing!

Cassia Harvey

©2020 C. Harvey Publications All Rights Reserved.

The Romberg Sonata in E Minor Practice Edition for Cello
Preparatory Exercises for Movement One

1. Fourth Position Notes and Bowing
Measures 1-3

©2020 C. Harvey Publications All Rights Reserved.

2a. Shifting Back 1/2 Step to D♯ - Top Fingering
Measure 4

2b. Shifting Back to Reach D♯ - Bottom Fingering
Measure 4

3. Finger Agility
Measures 7, 13, 14, 15

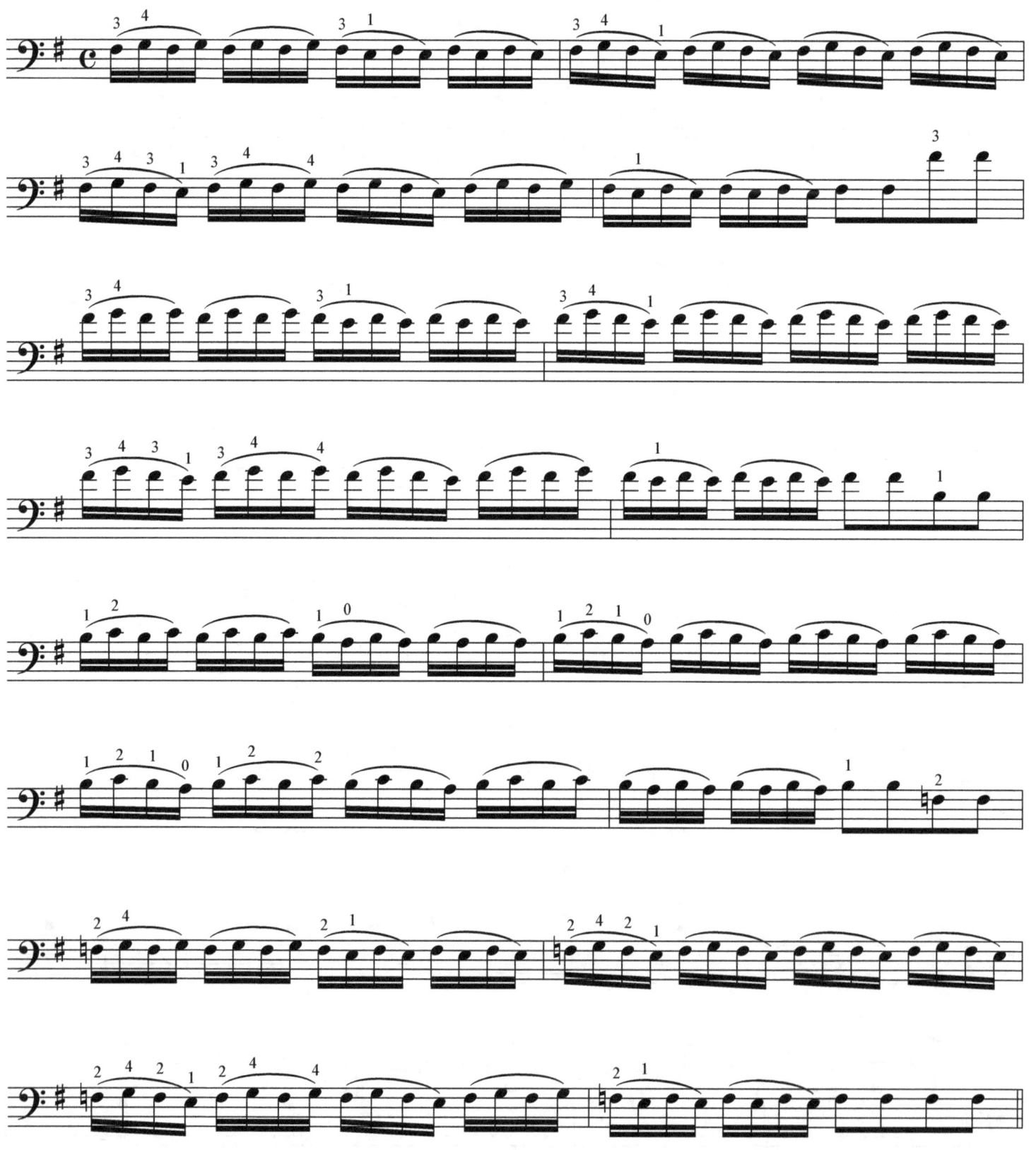

4. Agility and Bowing

Measure 7

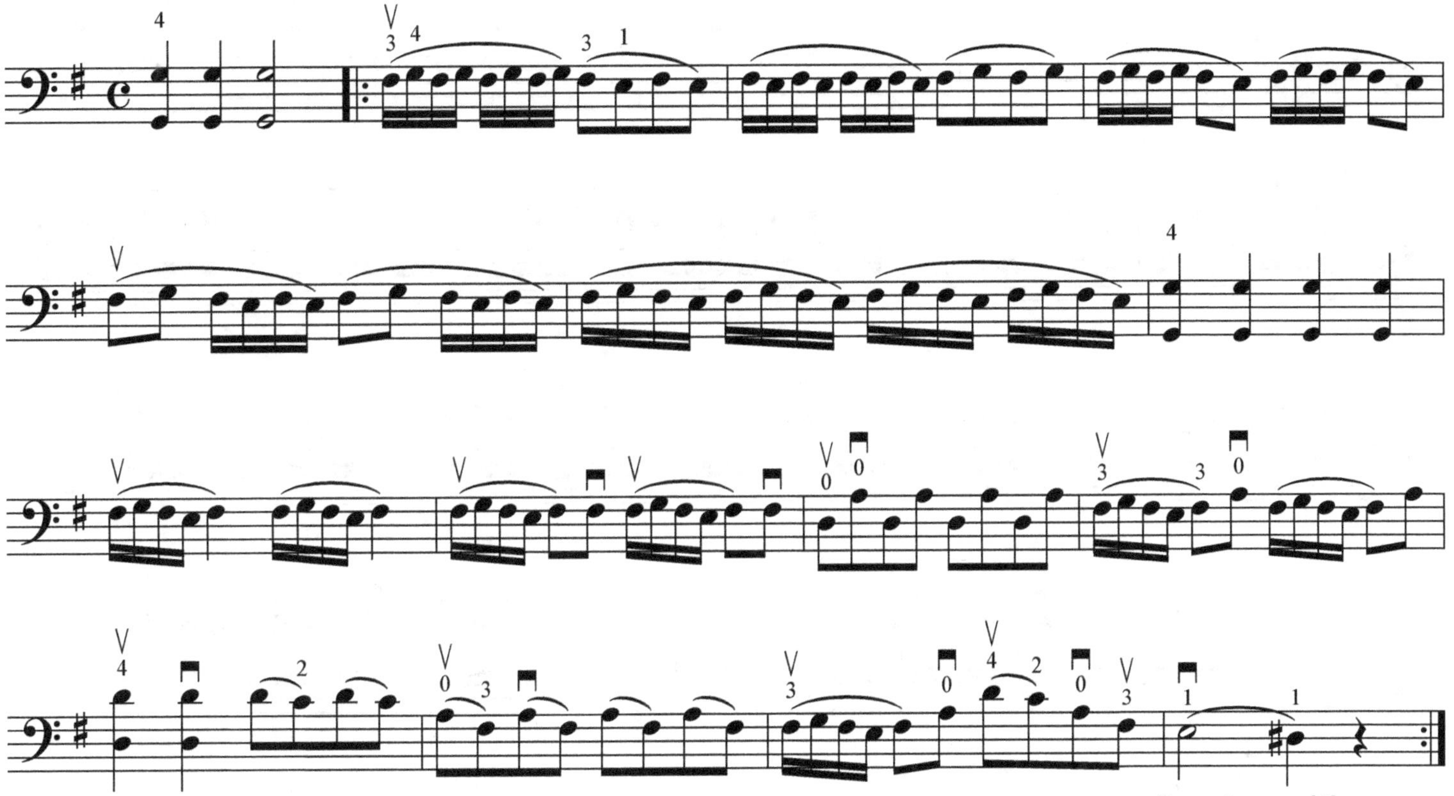

Repeat several times, playing faster each time.

5. Playing Across Strings

Measure 12

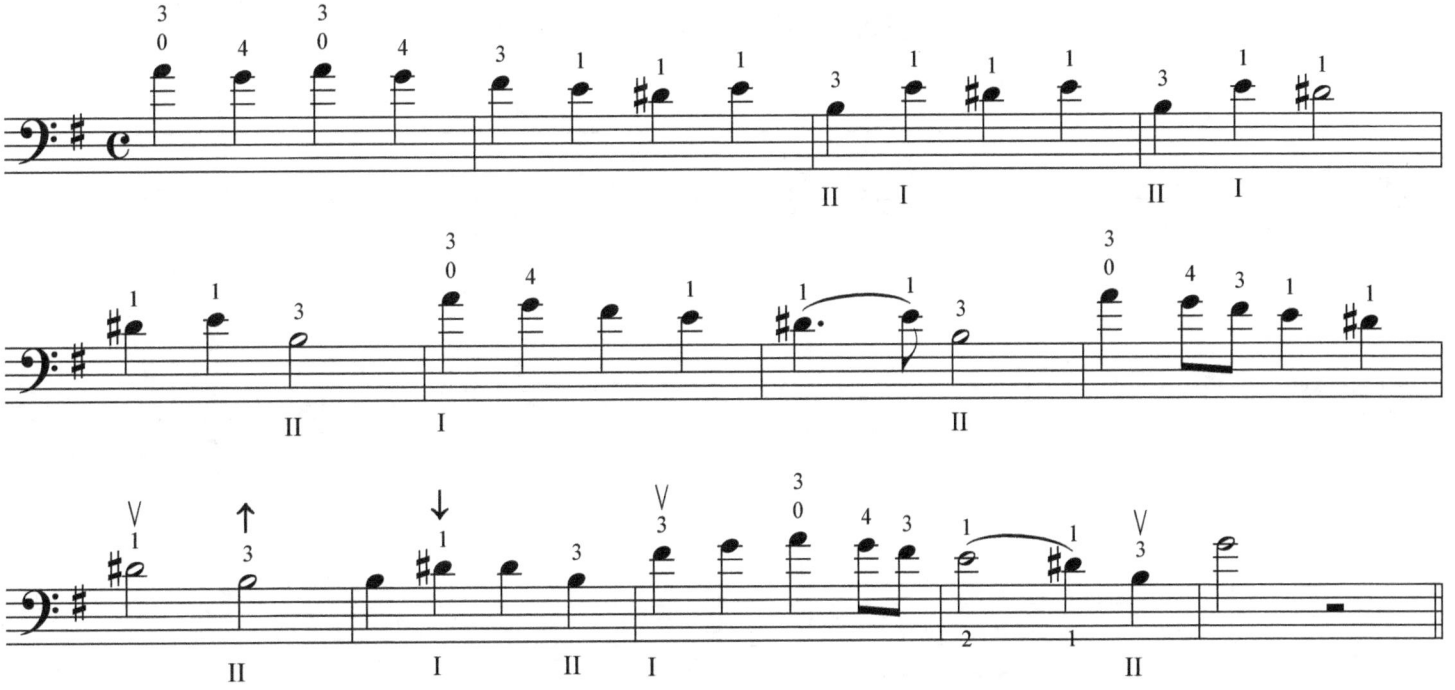

©2020 C. Harvey Publications All Rights Reserved.

6. Slow Up-Bows and Left-Hand Agility: Measure 13

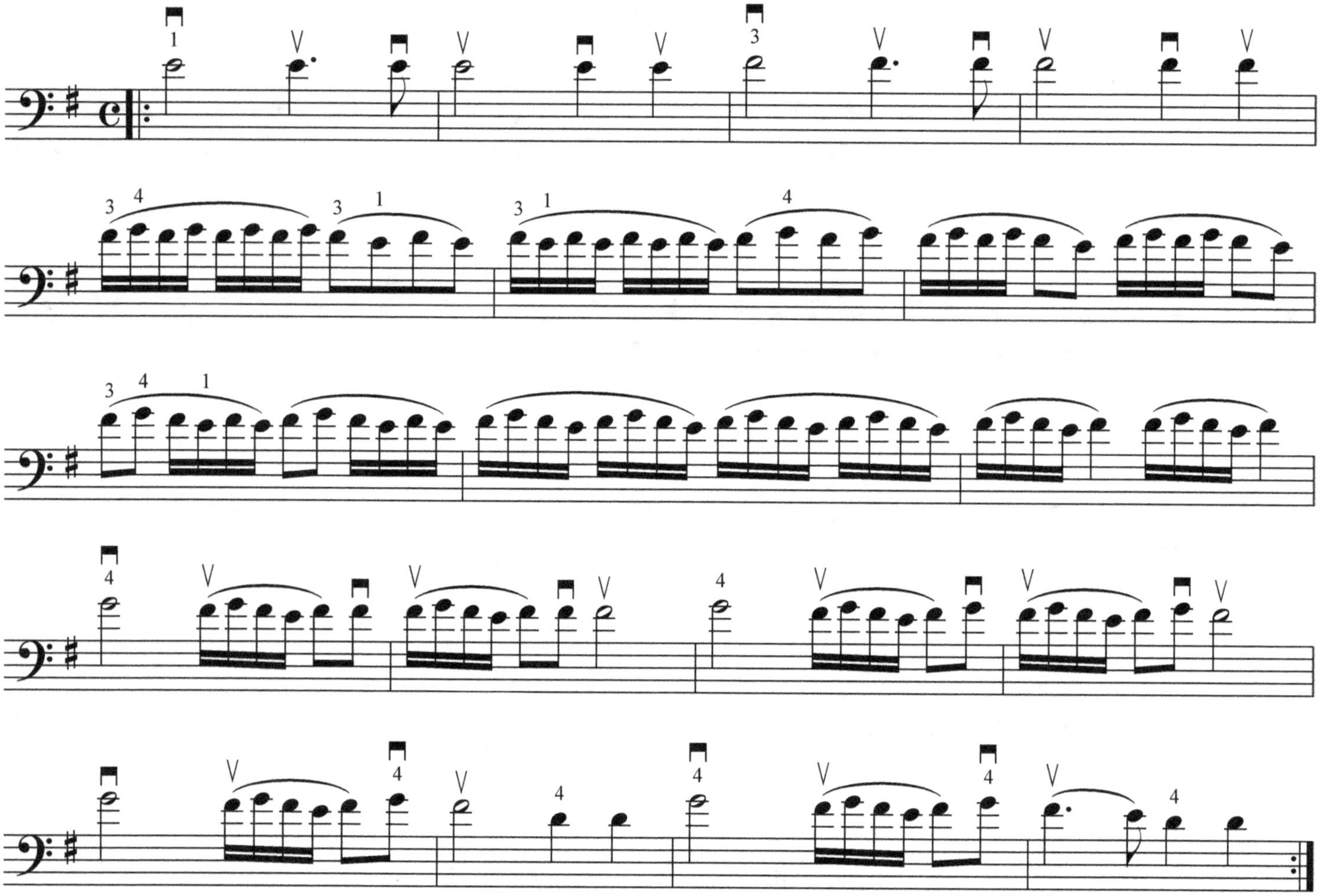

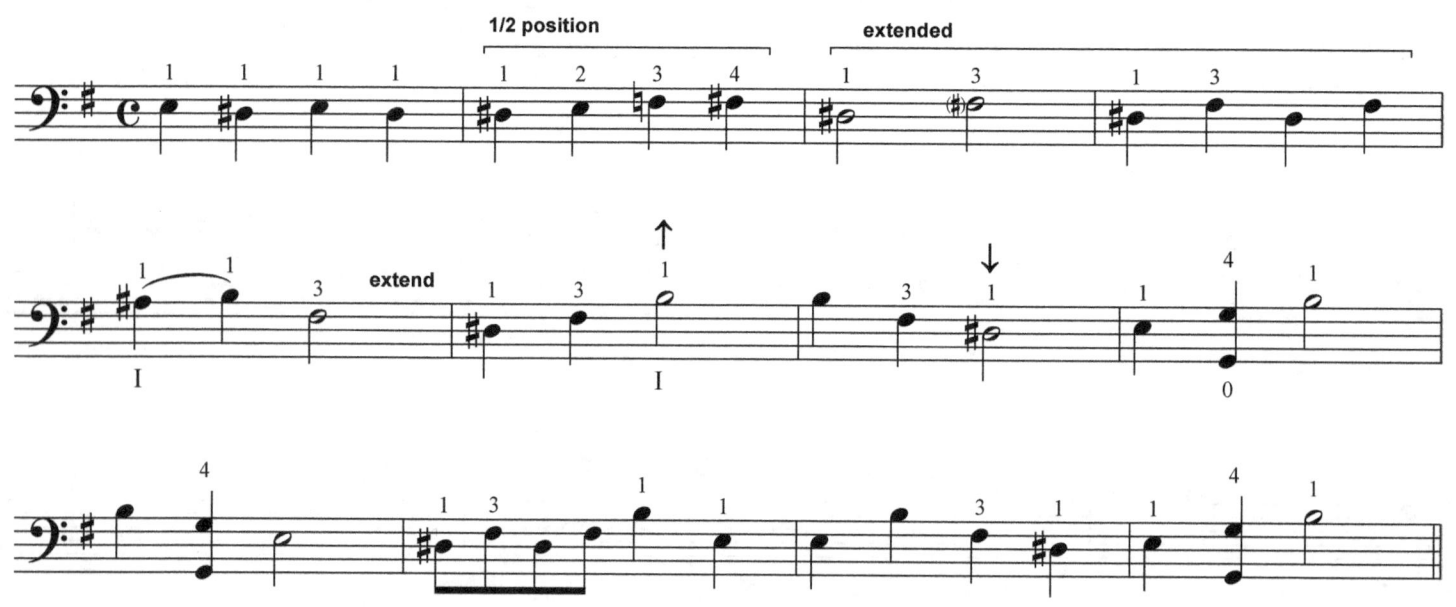

Repeat several times, playing faster each time.

7. Extending: Measures 19-21

©2020 C. Harvey Publications All Rights Reserved.

The Romberg Sonata in E Minor Practice Edition for Cello - Preparatory Exercises for Movement One

8. Shifting Into Second Position: Measures 23-25

9. Shifting to Second and Fourth Position: Measures 23-25

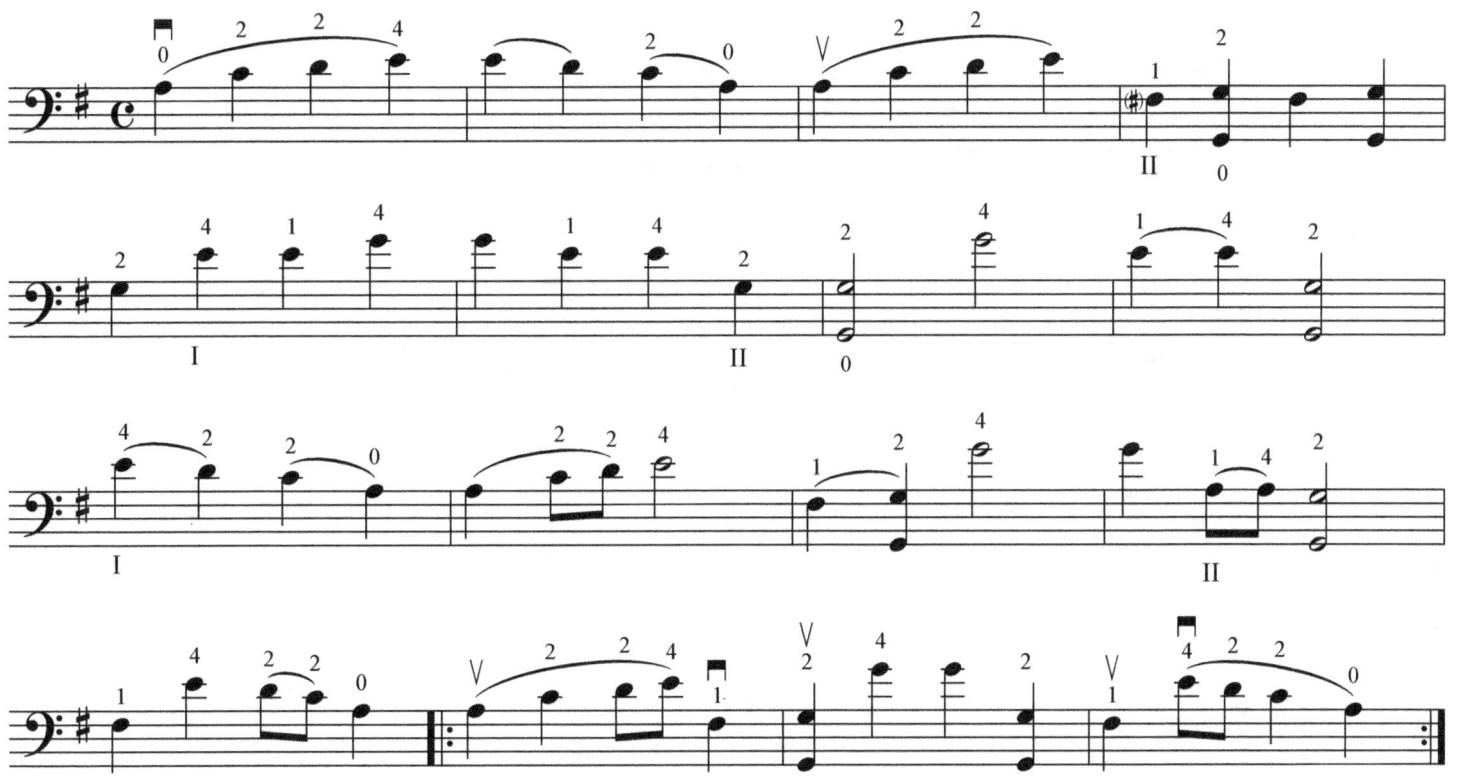

©2020 C. Harvey Publications   All Rights Reserved.

10. Rhythm and Bowing I
Measures 23-25

11. Rhythm and Bowing II
Measures 23-25

The Romberg Sonata in E Minor Practice Edition for Cello - Preparatory Exercises for Movement One

17

12. Finger Exercise with Open Strings
Measures 27-32

Repeat several times, playing faster each time.

13. Shifting and Bowing
Measure 40

©2020 C. Harvey Publications   All Rights Reserved.

The Romberg Sonata in E Minor Practice Edition for Cello - Preparatory Exercises for Movement One   21

©2020 C. Harvey Publications   All Rights Reserved.

What to Focus on in Movement One

- Play with long bows and a bold, strong tone.

- Play with curved fingers so that the string is stopped completely; this will give you the clearest sound.

- Focus on rhythm and counting correctly. This first movement has many different types of note values: whole notes, dotted half notes, half notes, dotted quarter notes, eighth notes, triplets, sixteenth notes, etc.

- Make sure you are following the bowings correctly even when it is awkward. Romberg seems to have cared a great deal about teaching bowing in his Sonatas and you can improve your bowing skills tremendously just by following his bowings.

24

I = A string
II = D string
III = G string
IV = C string

Movement One with Study Notes

B. Romberg
Arr. F. Jansen
Edited C. Harvey

Allegro non troppo: Lively but not too fast.
Study Tempo: ♩=72-88   Performance Tempo: ♩=92-132

©2020 C. Harvey Publications   All Rights Reserved.

The Romberg Sonata in E Minor Practice Edition for Cello - Movement One with Study Notes

The Romberg Sonata in E Minor Practice Edition for Cello - Movement One with Study Notes

28 The Romberg Sonata in E Minor Practice Edition for Cello
Preparatory Exercises for Movement Two

©2020 C. Harvey Publications   All Rights Reserved.

6. Learning the Notes: Measure 24

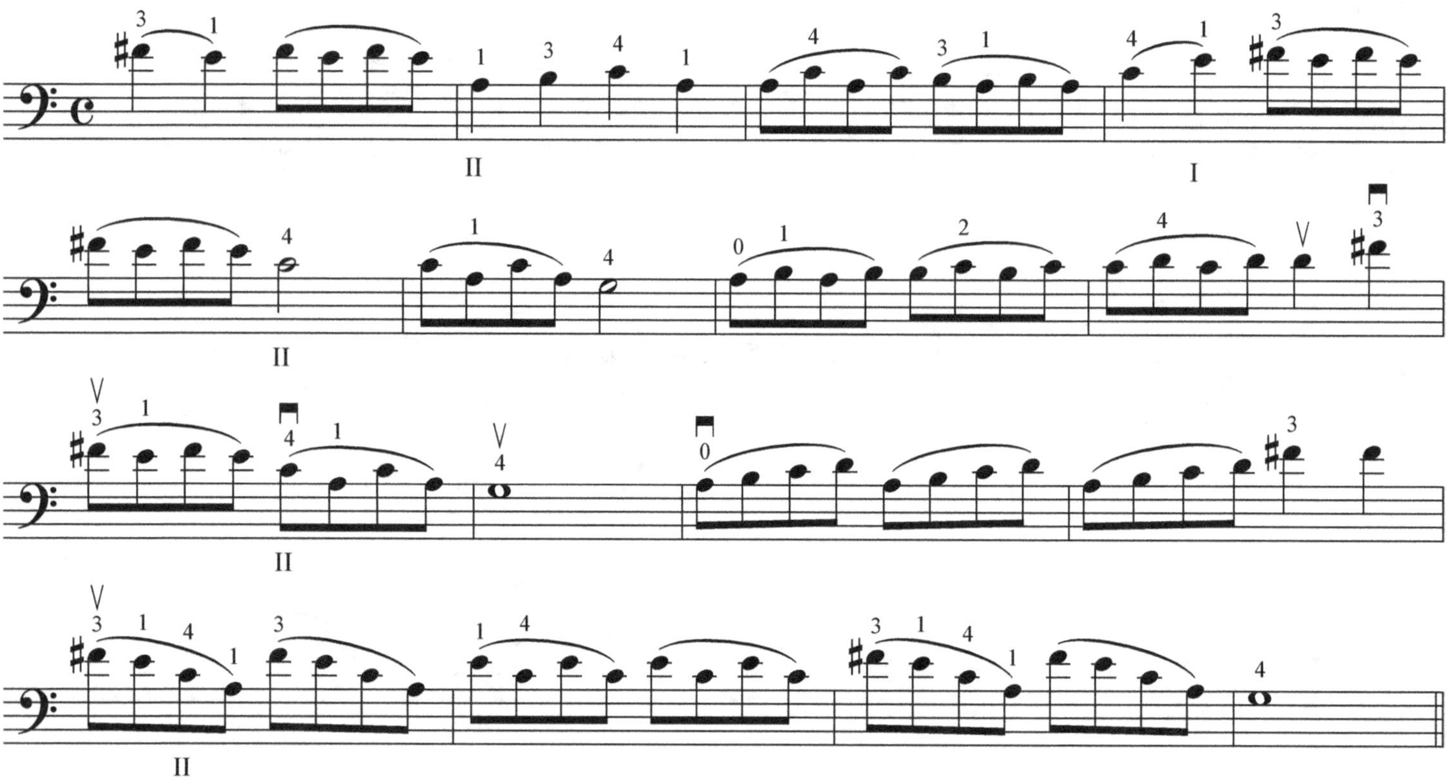

7. Learning the Fragments: Measure 24

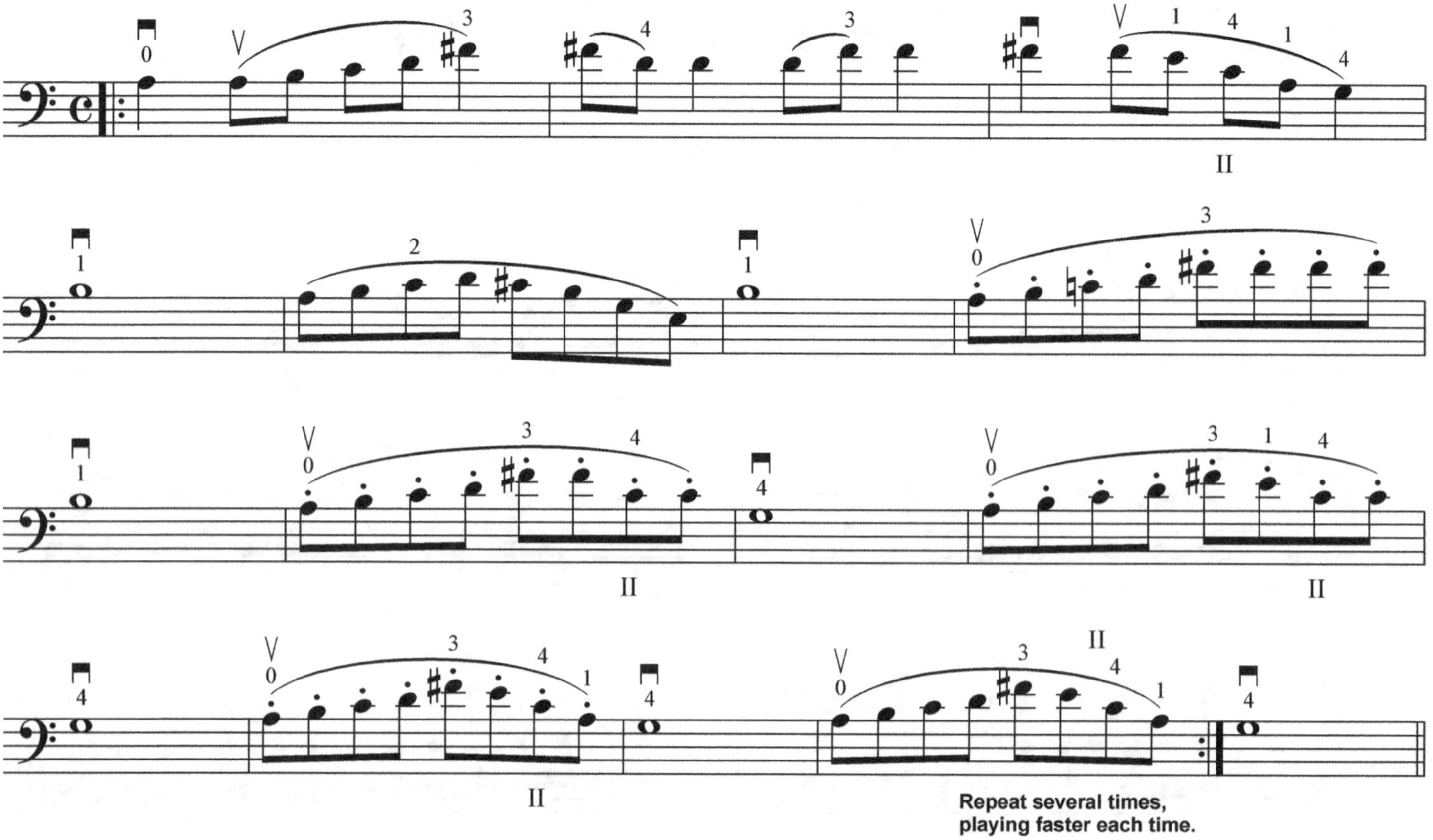

Repeat several times, playing faster each time.

The Romberg Sonata in E Minor Practice Edition for Cello - Preparatory Exercises for Movement Two

8. Working Towards Speed with Dotted Rhythms: Measure 24

Save your bow!

Repeat several times, playing faster each time.

9. Backwards and Forwards for Muscle Memory: Measure 24

Start slowly. Repeat this complete exercise several times, playing faster each time.

©2020 C. Harvey Publications   All Rights Reserved.

What to Focus on in Movement Two

- Play with long bows and a bold, strong tone.

- Play with curved fingers so that the string is stopped completely; this will give you the clearest sound.

- Focus on rhythm and counting correctly. This movement is best approached by counting in eighth notes; subdividing can help you properly place the thirty-second notes.

- In measure 23, keep your arm out to the side and your fingers curved so that you can shift up, and then across strings, quickly.

Movement Two (Written With Slower Note Values to Help Counting)

Please note: The note values *in relation to each other* are the same.

The Romberg Sonata in E Minor Practice Edition for Cello - Movement Two with Slower Notes Values

Movement Two with Study Notes

Andante grazioso: At a walking pace, gracefully

Study Tempo: ♪=80-96 (♩=40-48)
Performance Tempo: ♪=100-120 (♩=50-60)

The Romberg Sonata in E Minor Practice Edition for Cello - Movement Two with Study Notes 37

38 The Romberg Sonata in E Minor Practice Edition for Cello
Preparatory Exercises for Movement Three

1. The 3-2-1 Rhythm
Measures 6-7

2. Shifting
Measures 10-13

©2020 C. Harvey Publications   All Rights Reserved.

The Romberg Sonata in E Minor Practice Edition for Cello - Preparatory Exercises for Movement Three

40 The Romberg Sonata in E Minor Practice Edition for Cello - Preparatory Exercises for Movement Three

5. Shifting to 3rd Position: Measure 77

6. Shifting and Tenor Clef: Measures 77-78

©2020 C. Harvey Publications All Rights Reserved.

The Romberg Sonata in E Minor Practice Edition for Cello - Preparatory Exercises for Movement Three   41

7. Finding 7th Position: Measure 78

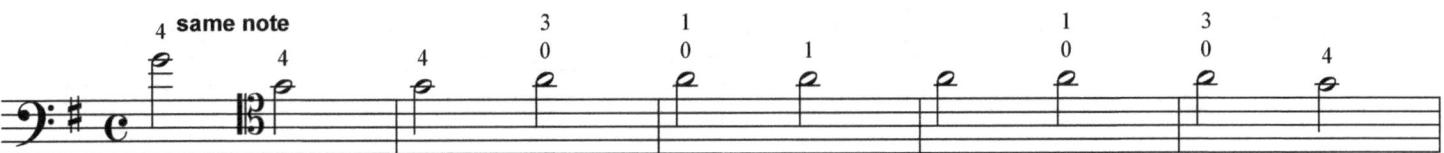

8. Spacing in 7th Position: Measure 78

Play this section 4 times.

9. Hearing the Notes: Measure 78

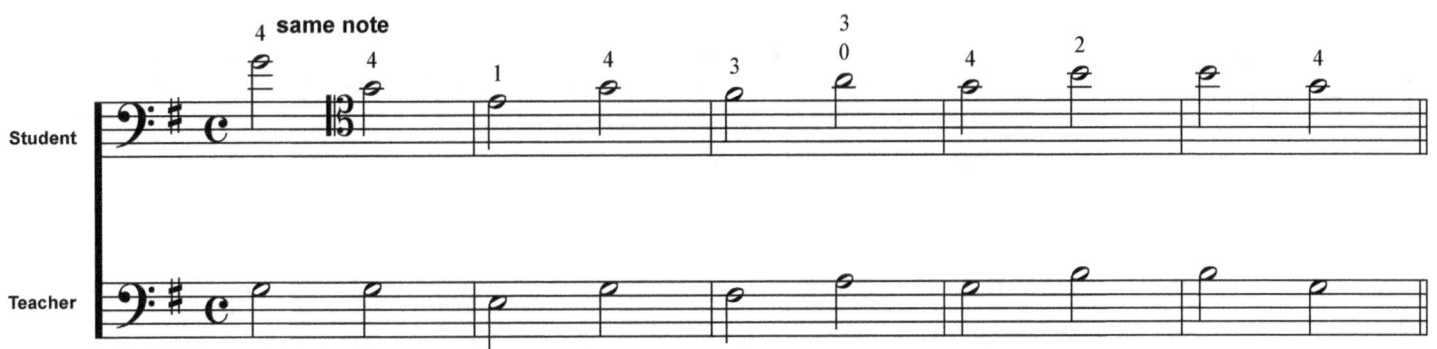

©2020 C. Harvey Publications   All Rights Reserved.

10. Shifting In and Out of 7th Position: Measure 78

11. Learning Third Finger: Measure 78

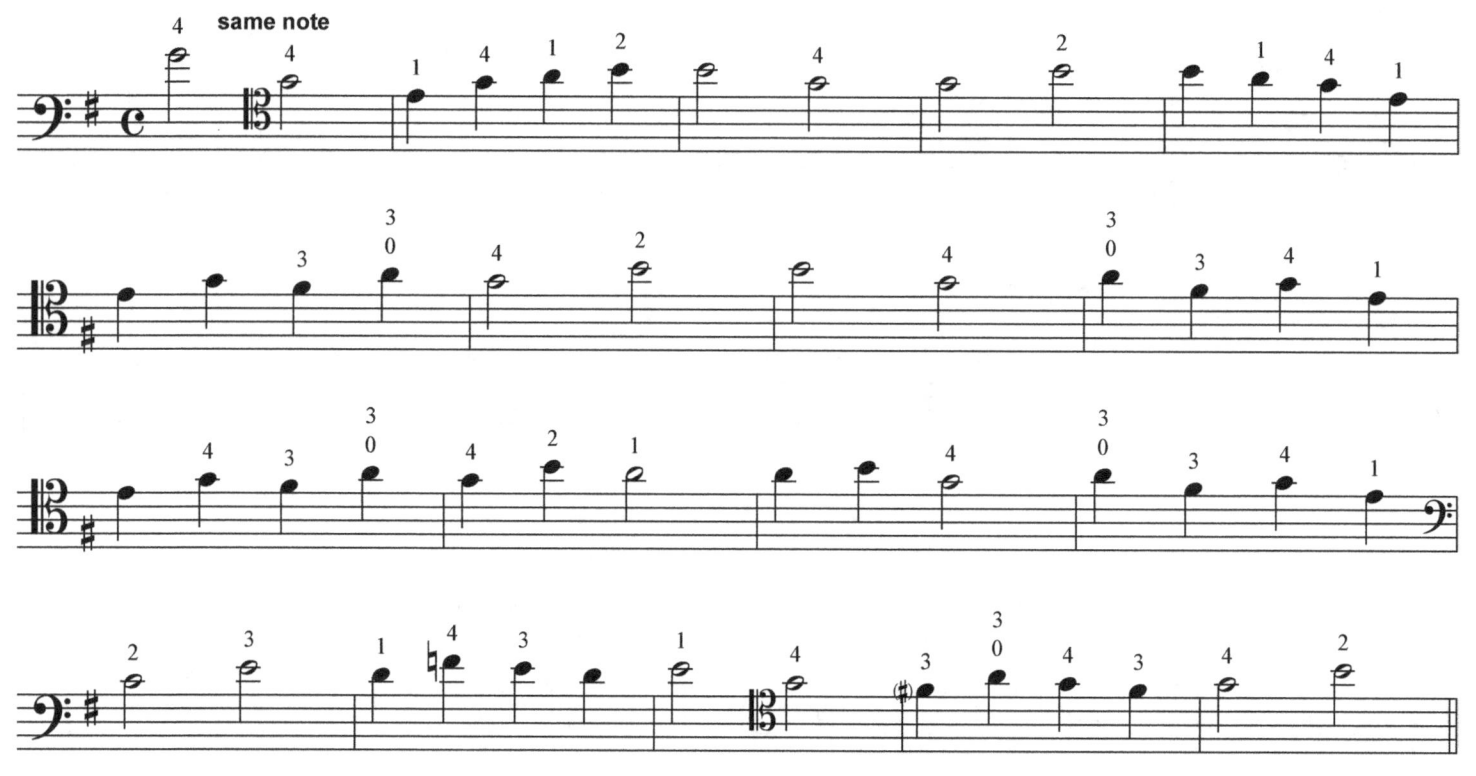

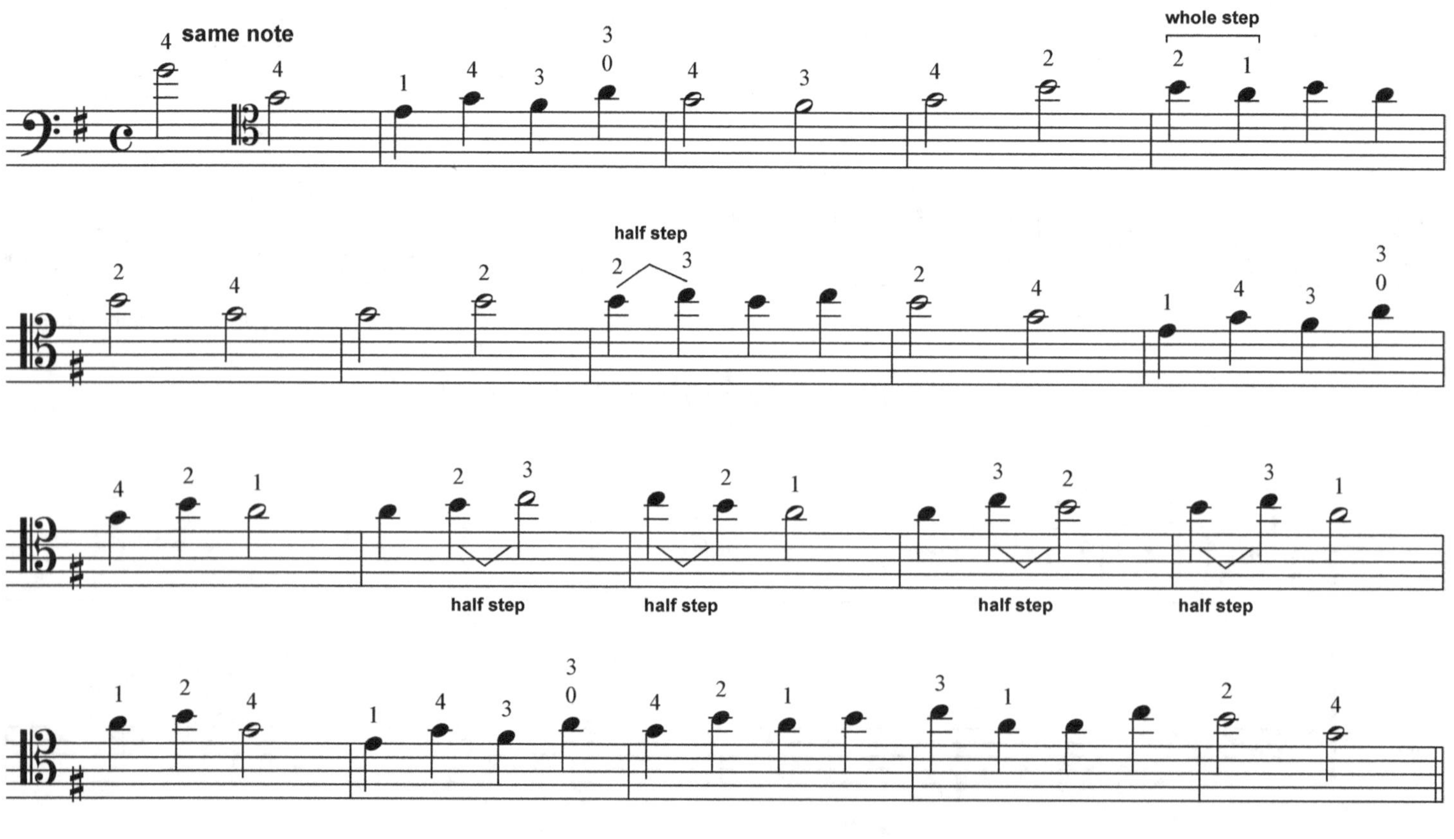

The Romberg Sonata in E Minor Practice Edition for Cello - Preparatory Exercises for Movement Three

12. Fluent Shifting
Measures 77-78

13. Shifting and Finger Agility
Measures 77-78

Repeat several times, playing faster each time.

14. Rhythmic Shifting
Measures 77-78

Repeat several times, playing faster each time.

©2020 C. Harvey Publications All Rights Reserved.

44

The Romberg Sonata in E Minor Practice Edition for Cello - Preparatory Exercises for Movement Three

15. Fluency and Speed: Measures 77-78

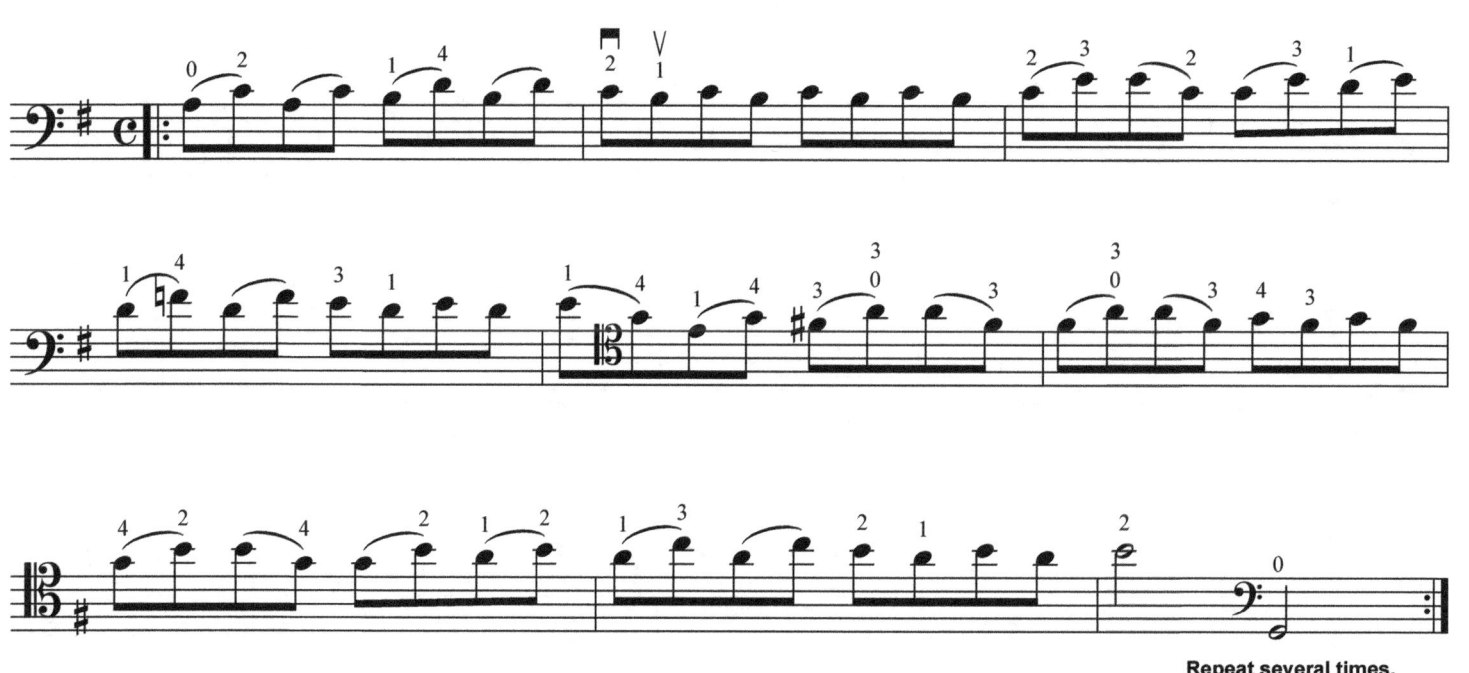

Repeat several times, playing faster each time.

16. Putting It All Together: Measures 77-78

©2020 C. Harvey Publications   All Rights Reserved.

The Romberg Sonata in E Minor Practice Edition for Cello - Preparatory Exercises for Movement Three

17. Saving the Bow
Measures 81-82

18. Shifting Across Strings
Measures 128-130

19. Bowing
Measures 131-133

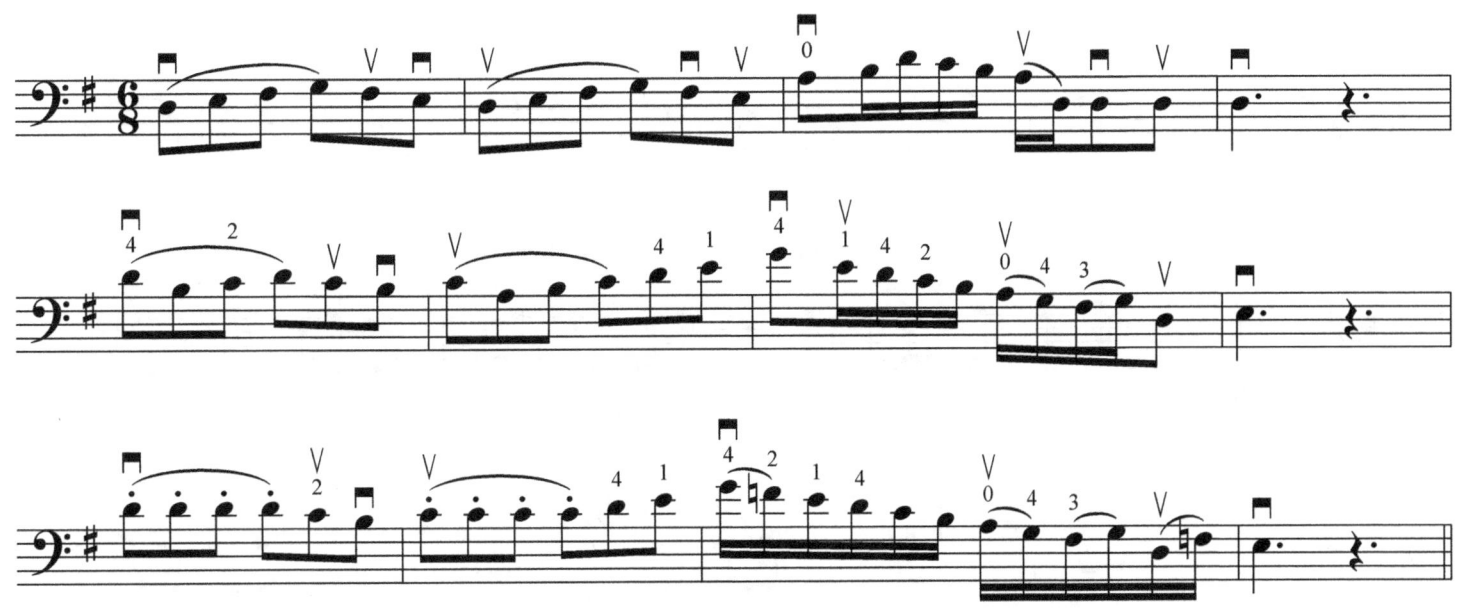

©2020 C. Harvey Publications   All Rights Reserved.

The Romberg Sonata in E Minor Practice Edition for Cello - Preparatory Exercises for Movement Three

20. Shifting I: Measures 134-136

21. Shifting II: Measures 137-141

©2020 C. Harvey Publications All Rights Reserved.

The Romberg Sonata in E Minor Practice Edition for Cello - Preparatory Exercises for Movement Three   47

22. Bowing I: Measures 150-153

23. Bowing II: Measures 154-157

©2020 C. Harvey Publications   All Rights Reserved.

48 The Romberg Sonata in E Minor Practice Edition for Cello - Preparatory Exercises for Movement Three

24. Shifting: Measures 167-170

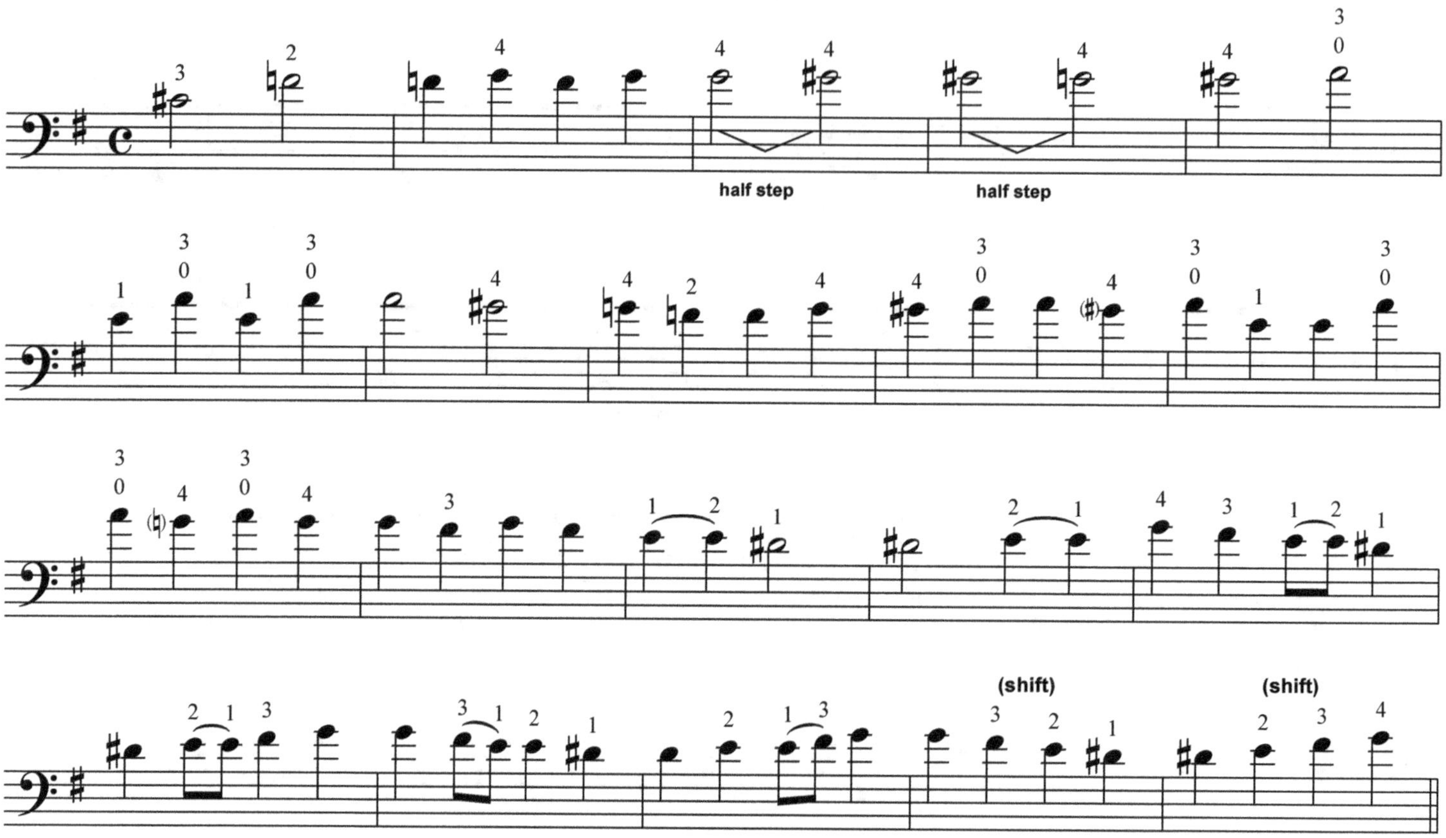

25. Bowing and Rhythm
Measures 210-218

©2020 C. Harvey Publications   All Rights Reserved.

What to Focus on in Movement Three

- Play with a bold, strong tone.

- Play with curved fingers so that the string is stopped completely; this will give you the clearest sound.

- Focus on rhythm and counting correctly. In this movement, the 3-2-1 (dotted quarter note, quarter note, eighth note) measures can often cause the most trouble. Be careful to count these measures very carefully:

- In the section where you need to shift into 7th position, make sure your arm and hand are above the side of the cello as you shift. Otherwise, you may get stuck as you shift or have trouble playing the high notes clearly.

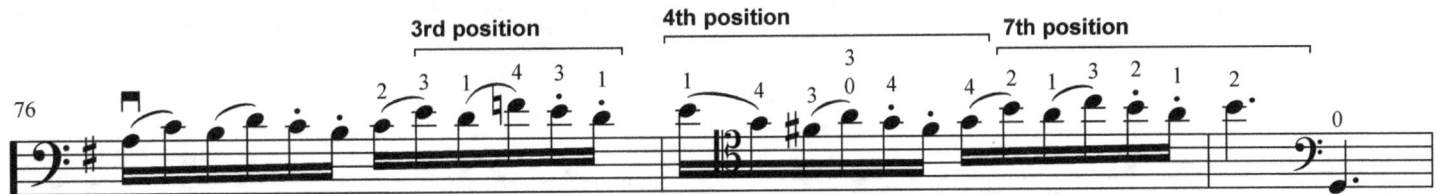

- In the string crossing sections, keep your wrist flexible and your fingers loose on the bow; the wrist and fingers should do most of the string crossing.

©2020 C. Harvey Publications All Rights Reserved.

Movement Three with Study Notes

Rondo: A form with a recurring main theme.
Allegretto: Moderately quick; slower than Allegro but faster than Andante.

Study Tempo: ♪=144-208   Performance Tempo: ♩.=69-84

The Romberg Sonata in E Minor Practice Edition for Cello - Movement Three with Study Notes

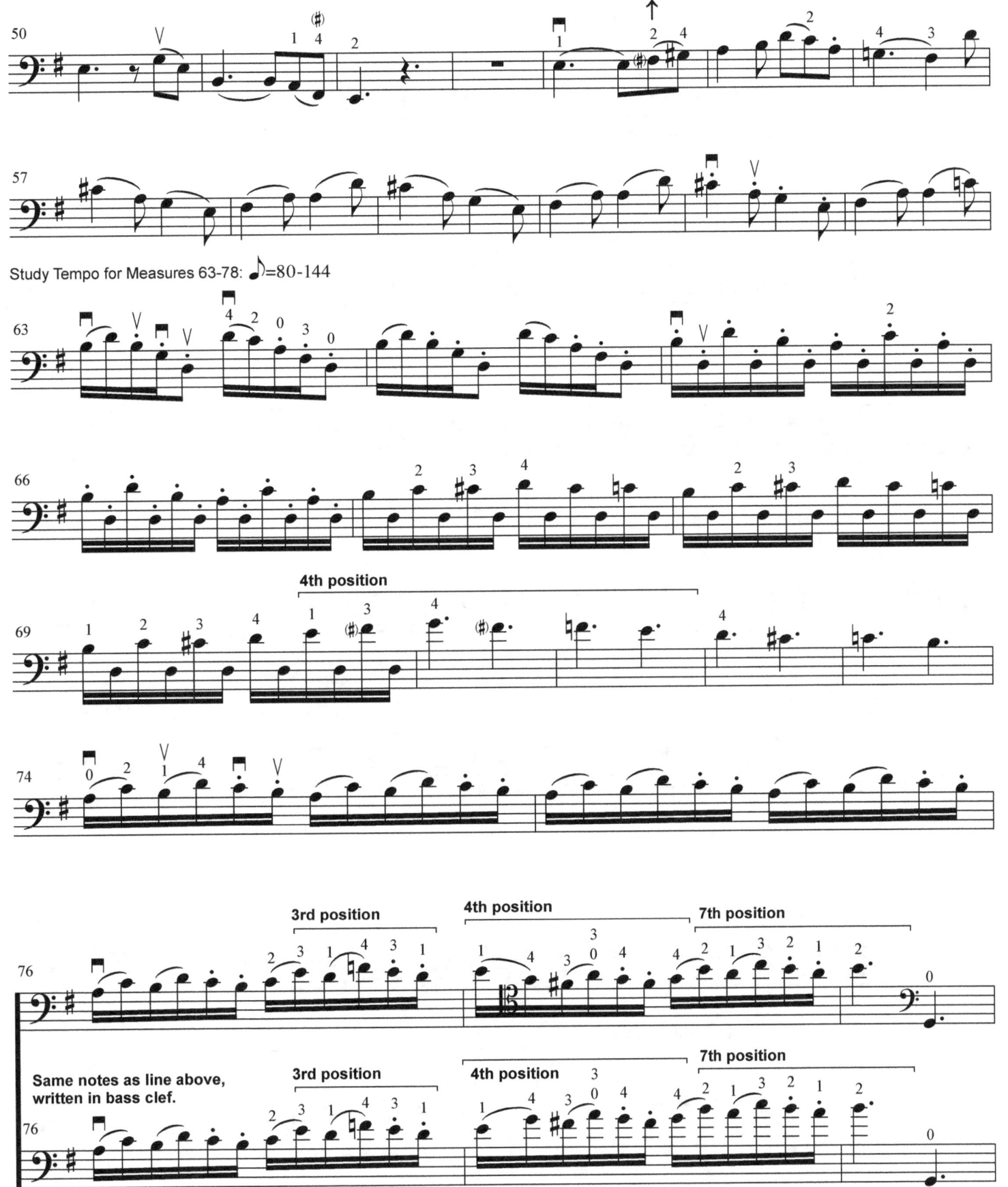

52 — The Romberg Sonata in E Minor Practice Edition for Cello - Movement Three with Study Notes

The Romberg Sonata in E Minor Practice Edition for Cello - Movement Three with Study Notes

The Romberg Sonata in E Minor Practice Edition for Cello - Movement Three with Study Notes

Sonata in E Minor

B. Romberg
Edited by F. Jansen, C. Harvey

Allegro non troppo

©2020 C. Harvey Publications All Rights Reserved.

The Romberg Sonata in E Minor Practice Edition for Cello - Complete Piece, Movement One

This page is left blank for page turns.

Andante grazioso

Rondo
Allegretto

The Romberg Sonata in E Minor Practice Edition for Cello - Complete Piece, Movement Three 63

The Romberg Sonata in E Minor Practice Edition for Cello - Complete Piece, Movement Three
65

Sonata in E Minor

B. Romberg, Arr. C. Harvey

Allegro non troppo

The Romberg Sonata in E Minor Practice Edition for Cello - Duet, Movement One

The Romberg Sonata in E Minor Practice Edition for Cello - Duet, Movement One

70 The Romberg Sonata in E Minor Practice Edition for Cello - Duet, Movement One

©2020 C. Harvey Publications   All Rights Reserved.

This page is left blank for page turns.

The Romberg Sonata in E Minor Practice Edition for Cello - Duet, Movement Two

Andante grazioso

©2020 C. Harvey Publications   All Rights Reserved.

The Romberg Sonata in E Minor Practice Edition for Cello - Duet, Movement Two

©2020 C. Harvey Publications All Rights Reserved.

74 — The Romberg Sonata in E Minor Practice Edition for Cello - Duet, Movement Three

Rondo Allegretto

The Romberg Sonata in E Minor Practice Edition for Cello - Duet, Movement Three

©2020 C. Harvey Publications All Rights Reserved.

The Romberg Sonata in E Minor Practice Edition for Cello - Duet, Movement Three

The Romberg Sonata in E Minor Practice Edition for Cello - Duet, Movement Three

©2020 C. Harvey Publications All Rights Reserved.

This page is left blank for page turns.

The Romberg Sonata in E Minor Practice Edition for Cello - Cello II Part, Movement Three

Rondo Allegretto

The Romberg Sonata in E Minor Practice Edition for Cello - Cello II Part, Movement Three

Sonata in E Minor

B. Romberg
Arranged by F. Jansen
Edited by C. Harvey

The Romberg Sonata in E Minor Practice Edition for Cello - Piano Accompaniment, Movement One 89

90

The Romberg Sonata in E Minor Practice Edition for Cello - Piano Accompaniment, Movement One

The Romberg Sonata in E Minor Practice Edition for Cello - Piano Accompaniment, Movement One 93

The Romberg Sonata in E Minor Practice Edition for Cello - Piano Accompaniment, Movement Two

©2020 C. Harvey Publications All Rights Reserved.

The Romberg Sonata in E Minor Practice Edition for Cello - Piano Accompaniment, Movement Three

The Romberg Sonata in E Minor Practice Edition for Cello - Piano Accompaniment, Movement Three 99

©2020 C. Harvey Publications All Rights Reserved.

The Romberg Sonata in E Minor Practice Edition for Cello - Piano Accompaniment, Movement Three 101

The Romberg Sonata in E Minor Practice Edition for Cello - Piano Accompaniment, Movement Three 103

©2020 C. Harvey Publications All Rights Reserved.

The Romberg Sonata in E Minor Practice Edition for Cello - Piano Accompaniment, Movement Three
105

Cello Curriculum Segments
When to Use the Romberg Sonata in a Course of Study

Step One

Methods
- Learning the Cello, Books One (CHP282) and Two (CHP287)
- String Builder, Book One (published Belwin)
- Essential Elements for Cello, Book One (published Hal Leonard)
- Suzuki Book One (if using a modified Suzuki approach) (published Summy-Birchard)

Exercises
- The Open-String Book for Cello (CHP182)
- Early Exercises for Cello (CHP183)
- Beginning Technique for Cello (CHP110)
- Double Stop Beginnings for Cello (CHP220)
- First Position Scale Studies for the Cello (CHP179)
- Playing in Keys for Cello (CHP242)
- Cello Stretching; Extended First Position (CHP243)

Supplements
- Cello Book One (CHP221)
- Playing the Cello, Book One (CHP300)

Repertoire Books
- Stepping Stones for Cello (published Boosey & Hawkes)
- Waggon Wheels for Cello (published Boosey & Hawkes)
- Solo Time for Strings, Book One (published Alfred)
- String Festival Solos, Book One (published Belwin)

Sonatas/Concertinos
- Reinagle Sonatina in G Major ((published Schott)
- Breval Concertino No. 4 in C Major, arr. Feuillard (published Delrieu)
- Schaffrath Sonata in G Major (published Schott)
- Matz Sonata da Camera (published Dominis Music)
- Breval Concertino No. 5 in D Major, arr. Feuillard (published Delrieu)

Note: Books published by C. Harvey Publications are noted with an item number (CHP101) and are available at www.charveypublications.com and/or www.learnstrings.com.

©2020 C. Harvey Publications All Rights Reserved.

Step Two: Early-Intermediate Level; Starting to Shift

Methods
- Fourth Position for the Cello (CHP131) or Fourth Position Study Book for Cello (CHPD078)
- Second Position for the Cello (CHP114)
- Third Position for the Cello (CHP116)
- Suzuki Books Two and Three (if using a modified Suzuki approach) (published Summy-Birchard)

Exercises
- Finger Exercises for Cello, Book One (CHP101)
- Open-String Bow Workouts for Cello, Book One (CHP351)

Supplements and Etudes
- Squire Twelve Easy Exercises (published Stainer and Bell)
- Dotzauer 113 Studies, Book One (published International)
- Flying Fiddle Duets for Two Cellos, Book One (CHP272)
- Playing the Cello, Book Two (CHP326)

Repertoire Books
- Solo Time for Strings, Book Two (published Alfred)
- String Festival Solos, Book Two (published Belwin)
- Pejtsik Violoncello Music for Beginners, Vol. 3, (published EMB)

Sonatas/Concertinos (in approximate order of study)
- Breval Sonata in C Major
- Marcello Sonata in E Minor (published International)

Note: Books published by C. Harvey Publications are noted with an item number (CHP101) and are available at www.charveypublications.com and/or www.learnstrings.com.

Step Three: Intermediate Level; Becoming Fluent in the Lower and Neck Positions

Methods
- Fifth Position for the Cello (CHP198)
- Suzuki Books Three, Four (if using a modified Suzuki approach) (published Summy-Birchard)
- Francesconi Scuola Pratica Del Violoncello (published Suvini Zerboni)

Exercises
- Serial Shifting for the Cello (CHP106)
- Finger Exercises for Cello, Book Two (CHP130)
- Double Stop Etudes for the Cello (CHP202)

Scales
- The Two Octaves Book for Cello (CHP122)

Supplements and Etudes
- Schroeder 170 Foundation Studies, Vol. 1 (published Carl Fischer)
- Flying Fiddle Duets for Two Cellos, Book Two (CHP309)

Short Pieces
- Squire Bourree (published Carl Fischer)
- Squire Tarantella (published Carl Fischer)

Bach
- The Bach Cello Suite No. 1 Study Book (CHP332)

Sonatas/Concertos (in approximate order of study)
- **Romberg Sonata in E Minor (this book)**
- Romberg Sonata in C Major Study Book (CHP348)
- Goltermann Concerto No. 4 Study Book for Cello (CHP364)

Note: Books published by C. Harvey Publications are noted with an item number (CHP101) and are available at www.charveypublications.com and/or www.learnstrings.com, as well as where you purchased this book.

©2020 C. Harvey Publications All Rights Reserved.

Step Four: Late-Intermediate Level; Adding Tenor Clef and the Higher Positions

Methods
- De'ak Modern Method for the Cello, Book Two (published Presser)
- Tenor Clef for the Cello (CHP109)
- Suzuki Book Five (if using a modified Suzuki approach) (published Summy-Birchard)

Exercises
- The Shifting Book for Cello, Part One (CHP171) and Part Two (CHP172)
- Shifting in Keys for Cello, Book One (CHP244)
- Double Stop Shifting for Cello (CHP219)
- Octave Shifts for the Cello, Book One (CHP104)
- Finger Exercises for Cello, Book Three (CHP142)

Scales
- Learning Three-Octave Scales on the Cello (CHP356)
- The C Major Scale Book for Cello (CHP117)
- Arpeggio Studies in Two Octaves for Cello (CHP155)

Supplements and Etudes
- Feuillard 60 Etudes for the Young Cellist (published Delrieu)
- Schroeder 170 Foundation Studies, Vol. 2 (published Carl Fischer)
- Lee 40 Melodic and Progressive Etudes, Vol. 1 (Published Schirmer)

Short Pieces
- Squire Danse Rustique (published Carl Fischer)
- Saint-Saens The Swan Study Book (CHP346)
- Saint-Saens Allegro Appassionato (published Carl Fischer)
- Faure Elegie Study Book (CHP319)

Bach
- Bach Cello Suites No. 2,3 (published Barenreiter as 6 Suites for Solo Violoncello)

Sonatas/Concertos (in approximate order of study)
- Klengel Concertino in C Major (published International)
- Romberg Sonata in G Major, Op. 43, No. 3 (published International)

Note: Books published by C. Harvey Publications are noted with an item number (CHP101) and are available at www.charveypublications.com and/or www.learnstrings.com.

©2020 C. Harvey Publications All Rights Reserved.

Also Available from C. Harvey Publications

The Romberg Sonata in C Major Study Book for Cello
CHP348

- Exercises are included to teach you every measure.
- Essential cello technique is distilled and presented.
- The complete cello part to the Sonata is included.
- Master the Sonata that comes after the Romberg Sonata in E Minor!

www.charveypublications.com - print books
www.learnstrings.com - downloadable books

©2020 C. Harvey Publications   All Rights Reserved.